If not now…

If not now…

Poems by

Anita Barrows

© 2022 Anita Barrows. All rights reserved.
This material may not be reproduced in any form, published,
reprinted, recorded, performed, broadcast,
rewritten or redistributed without
the explicit permission of Anita Barrows.
All such actions are strictly prohibited by law.

Cover design by Shay Culligan
Cover photograph by Andrew Lehman

ISBN: 978-1-63980-137-4

Kelsay Books
502 South 1040 East, A-119
American Fork, Utah 84003
Kelsaybooks.com

For Nora and Viva, Ciel and Dashiell

Acknowledgment

"Alphabet Poem" previously appeared in *Tikkun Magazine,* Fall 2015.

Alphabet Poem

    for my students
    and in memory of Sandra Bland

(a)

The difference between my life and yours
is this: When I was pulled over once by a cop
for running a stop sign, and before
he got to my car I'd taken my phone
out of my purse to let my kid know
I'd be late coming home, what the cop did
was warn me not to be digging my hand
in my purse with a cop's face
in the driver's window. The difference
between my life and yours
is that I put the phone
back and sat looking out at the traffic
while the cop wrote the ticket, and in the end
I got home only twenty minutes
later than I had promised.

(b)

Do you think I'm at peace with this?
A woman I know and her dog
saw a man shot in the back
by a cop at the end of the block
they live on, and for no reason.
They were walking and suddenly their block
became a warfield. Before that,
she had thought of the day as simple.

Before that, she had been planning
just to go home, take the leash
off the dog, make coffee,
put on her yellow sweater.

(c)

Then the police were everywhere.
Then it became a question
of what she had seen
and how many times she could tell it.
Then it was clear that her life
had become this man, who was dead.

(d)

There were cameras and people cleaning the street
of his blood, which was everywhere.
It didn't seem possible that so much blood
could have come from a single body.
Even when the ambulance took him away
it seemed the blood kept flowing.
It flowed from the stores, the doorways.
It flowed from the hydrants that should have been filled with water.
Even by afternoon, everyone
who set foot on that block had begun to bleed.

(e)

The difference between my life and yours
is that our bleeding is exactly the same.

(f)

All day the dog lay in the corner of the kitchen.
Anything that passed with a loud noise,
the dog, who had been a confident, placid dog,
startled. Stood up and walked in circles. Growled.
Went searching from room to room
for his person, who was no longer
there, who had become
that other person.

(g)

My kid didn't really care that I came home late.
She was watching her favorite program.
She was sitting in front of the tv
eating cold macaroni and cheese
with a spoon, and I yelled at her
because if I had been you I might have
been killed by the cop
for trying to make that call
on a phone the cop
might have said
was a weapon. And there she was,
not even bothering to look up when I walked in the door,

sitting in the armchair, legs folded under her,
mac and cheese in a blue plastic cereal bowl,
laughing at something one character said to another.

(h)

She didn't know his name at first.
He was just one more person shot in the back.
The cops rifled through his pockets.
It looked like they were even touching his dick
but he couldn't feel it.
She heard his name spoken later on the radio,
found out that he had two kids and a mother.

(i)

She did what she could about the bleeding,
used every bit of gauze and adhesive in the apartment,
wondered whether she should go
to the ER when it didn't stop by late
afternoon, but how
could she go when they had him
already listed as DOA
and they wouldn't understand
that she was him now, and in need of help?

(j)

It wasn't just her. It was everyone on the block.
At night, when people began to turn on their lamps
and she could see through their windows, she realized
that everyone was bandaging themselves
or bandaging others they lived with.
And those already swaddled in bandages were mopping up blood.

(k)

The difference between my life and yours
is that, even though I reached for my phone,
I still went to bed that night in my pajamas
and woke up in the morning. You, if you
had reached for your phone in the same
situation, would have been lying there
in the road by that stop sign, and no one
would have known if you had a kid at home
eating mac and cheese straight out of the fridge
and waiting, waiting.

(l)

The police came to her door and asked her again.
She told them what she had told them before.
They said that everyone on the block had told them
the same story and still they didn't believe it.
They were waiting for one person to say something different.
It had grown cold outside. Rivulets of frozen blood
stuck to the carpet in the hallway of the building.

The police thought they were threads of polyester
and when they looked at them that was what they became.
Afterward they thawed. The smell of blood was unmistakable.

(m)

It's important to consider the dog.
He was not a watchdog. Some of his ancestors
had been herding dogs, and because of that
it was his nature to want everyone
in the same place.

(n)

It bothered me that my kid was being so lazy.
I mean, who taught her it was ok to eat mac and cheese
without heating it up? In the microwave
it takes no time at all. And the fact
that she didn't even
look up, not until the next commercial.
I mean, if I were you I might have been dead.

(o)

To give her the benefit of the doubt,
she had no idea.
And why would she? If I said I was coming home,
I was coming home.
That's the difference. The kid could count on it.

(p)

Am I saying this to you? Am I saying it to myself?
The kid   could count   on her mother   coming home

(q)

Nothing else looked the same either.
All the faces on the block had become his face.
Everyone, even the next morning,
when everything had already been cleaned up
and the newspaper was already reporting
that someone new had been shot by police,
even then you could see the place on everyone's back,
where their shirt was torn, where the flesh
under their shirt was torn.

(r)

He had two kids and a mother.
The mother was a woman who went to church
and that was where she went that day and the next day
while a neighbor babysat.
The kids? They went back
to school after a few days
of sitting watching
their grandma cry on the phone
and had to tell their friends
that their dad was dead. Some
of their friends had dead
dads too.

(s)

At the funeral his kids wore blue dresses
and sat with their grandma
in the front row. It was a little
like regular church and a little like a school assembly,
and afterward when they went back
to where they lived there was no dad again.
Meanwhile, in the apartment building, rivulets of blood kept
flowing.

(t)

She began to think she could hear the crying of his kids at night.
She had learned they were girls. She had learned
a few other things, too: they were seven and five
and their names rhymed. At night she lay in her bed
thinking of names that would rhyme with theirs.
Still, every morning, because of the blood,
she had to throw out the sheets.

(u)

She noticed that others who lived on the block
were doing the same.
The dumpsters were filled with bloody sheets.
There seemed to be no way to wash the blood out.

(v)

Do you know how lucky you are to have a mother
I wanted to yell at her, but I kept my mouth shut
about everything besides the cold mac and cheese.
After all she's only a kid. All her life
she's had everything she needed. Her name
doesn't rhyme with *death* or *blood* or *gunshot wound* or *police*.

(w)

So I sat down next to her in the armchair and watched the rest of
the program.

(x)

Within weeks the city had passed an ordinance
against bloody sheets in the dumpsters.
There was no room anymore for normal garbage.

(y)

She looked around at all the torn flesh.
It was all still bleeding and maybe it would bleed forever.
It occurred to her that they could wind all the sheets
together, make a rope of them, or an altar.

(z)

The dog too had begun to bleed.
He was less nervous now, but a small hole had bloomed in his back
under his tawny-colored fur. When she walked him
now in the mornings, others walked with them or followed.
No one spoke. A wake of blood streamed behind them.
It seemed like a kind of procession.

Would You Harbor Them?

for Amanda, Justin and Mabel
and in memory of Elijah McClain

(1)

Lie on cool grass, look up at the leaves
Maple and sycamore of your childhood
Summer after summer after summer
Sunlight filtering through them

(2)

My friends tell me this
while their infant, three months,
lies in her carriage, looking up
at the broad leaves of the fig tree:

It was a day
when helicopters
circled the city, one after another

The sound, after weeks of quarantine,
startling, deafening
In the streets, people marching
Thousands downtown, thousands walking
down the main avenues
This must end These killings must end

(3)

And if not now,
when?

(4)

What the kids heard was a knock at the door
They were sitting in the living room finishing schoolwork
It was the last week of online school for the year
The twelfth week of Shelter in Place
The younger one—ten—
was cutting construction paper to make hats
Graduation hats for his fifth grade class
Later the teacher would come to their steps
to get them, drop one off
at each of the homes of her fifth grade students
This is how it happens in these times
This is how we are learning to do it

(5)

I have been thinking this morning about Elijah McClain
who played his violin for the caged dogs at the Pound
Who wouldn't eat meat, who wouldn't kill insects
Who went out one evening in August
and was murdered by police
for wearing a ski mask (he was
anemic, subject
to feeling chilled), looking, as
someone who'd made the call said, "suspicious."

I am thinking now of the dogs—lonely
abandoned. Old dogs nobody wants, pit bull mixes
nobody wants. I am thinking of them circling,
settling, at last lying down
on the towels set out for them
on the concrete floors of their cages. Listening

(6)

It's a woman standing outside the door.
in sweatpants and a tank top.
Helicopters circle overhead
The noise they make muffles the sound
of her knocking.
She knocks once, twice
It's chilly outside: fog-chilly, wind-chilly,
though it's late spring
Her arms uncovered
Her shoes, rubber flip-flops
She's cold and she's tired and she's been walking
a long time and she's
shivering and she's
afraid

(7)

She says this when the older child—
fifteen—comes to the door.
Later the girl will say she thought
it was her brother's teacher knocking.

The woman at the door says she's afraid
They're following me, she says
Who, the girl asks
Not *What's your name?* Not *Why
are you here?* Not *What
are you doing knocking on my door*
But *Who? Who's following you?*

(8)

Paper hats
Construction paper folded in triangles
Stickers on them—stars, rainbows, unicorns
The kitchen table strewn with markers, tape
The boy quietly folding
His sister with buds in her ears, rocking slightly
to the music

(9)

I have to tell you: the boy,
his sister, his mother
are White
Not Black like the woman who comes to the door
It's days after George Floyd was murdered
in Minneapolis by police
It's a Tuesday afternoon in west Berkeley
in the month of June, 2020

(10)

The girl, without
removing her earbuds, tells the woman
to come inside. The woman is shaking
and repeating, over
and over, *They're following me.* By now
the children's mother,
who had been in the basement putting laundry
in the dryer, is up in the living room.
(I have to remind you
that we are in the twelfth week
of Shelter in Place. Anyone
can have this virus. Anyone
can transmit this virus
to anyone else. There are people
who have never, in all these weeks,
allowed anyone who doesn't live
in their home to enter.)
The mother looks at the woman
standing inside her living room.
My name is Carla, she tells her,
These are my children, Julie and Will

(11)

Elijah McClain lies on the street,
the police beating him. He is crying
and they are mocking him. He is pleading with them:
I'm different, I'm an introvert, I don't fight.

I'm thinking about the dogs listening in their cages
to Elijah playing his violin. Sometimes now
when I am playing Simpson, Dowland,
on my bass viola da gamba, I watch
the youngest, most boisterous, of my dogs
climb onto the couch, rest his head
on the cushion, calm. *I play this in honor
of Elijah McClain,* I tell myself. *Murdered at twenty-three.*

(12)

I am fifty years older than Elijah McClain
when he died. I have had children, grandchildren.
Every day I play my viola da gamba.
Every day I take long walks with my dogs.
Like Elijah McClain, I don't eat meat.
I sit on my back porch during Shelter in Place, doing my work,
and watch sunlight filter through leaves.
My body is not full of contusions.
I have not died on a dark street at the hands of police

(13)

The woman cannot stop talking about being followed
but the children's mother offers her a sweater
and she accepts it. Also a cup of tea and some cookies.
At last she is calm enough to sit down on the couch
and the children's mother sits down next to her.
The orders order us not to sit
on a couch in your living room

next to a woman you have never seen before
who has knocked on your door, come into your house.
Who is being followed from outside herself or from inside,
by police or by history

(14)

The woman tells them her name is Isha.
She has been walking a long time. She does not
remember where she began. She says something
about a nephew, something about a place
she thinks she had been staying at. She has no phone,
no papers. *We'll help you, Isha*, Carla says.
And she takes the first step—no, maybe
the second—off some kind of grid, into
some kind of unknown

(15)

Two women are sitting and talking
on a couch in west Berkeley
on a June afternoon during Shelter in Place.
Helicopters still circle the city.
The boy is still folding paper hats.
His sister sits in the armchair texting a friend

(16)

Isha says she would like to help the boy
make the paper hats. He hands her
scissors, construction paper.
Carla is folding laundry, stacks
of t-shirts, underwear, on the couch
they had been sitting on.
The girl is still texting her friend.
Every once in a while she laughs
at something we don't know about

(17)

When I was a child the woman who cleaned our house
had three daughters around my age.
Cynthia, Annette, and Jeanette,
On holidays, when she still
had to come to work, she would have to bring them.
She couldn't leave them alone in their Rockaway apartment.
My mother required that they stay in the basement.
My mother would not allow me to play with them.
We don't play with their kind, my mother would say.
I would sneak downstairs when my mother
would leave the house to go to the hairdresser.
I knew it would take a number of hours.
I would bring scissors downstairs, paper dolls.
Cynthia, Annette and Jeanette and I
would sit on the linoleum floor
of the basement, dressing the dolls, laughing.
Giving them names

(18)

Isha likes making the hats.
She and Will are talking. The boy
is telling Isha about the friends
he hasn't seen in twelve weeks.
Carla is making a phone call
to Social Services
to see if she can find a shelter
for Isha, to see if maybe
they have her listed somehow
with some address, since Isha still
can't remember where she started
walking from. The man who answers the phone
at Social Services says he cannot help, it's too late
in the day, Social Services
is about to close. He tells Carla
to call the police. Carla
tells him goodbye. When she
gets off the phone
she says to everyone assembled,
There is no way on this earth I would call the police

(19)

Who was it who called the police
on Elijah McClain?

(20)

We know the dangers of this virus.
There are other dangers

(21)

In the kitchen there is a bed
where the children like to curl up with blankets
on chilly days. It's a bed
that used to be in one of the children's rooms
before their mother and father divorced.
Everything changed in the house after that,
like having a bed in the kitchen. Like
opening the door and letting a woman in
whom you never have seen before
while a virus is raging. While helicopters
are raging

(22)

Isha sits at the kitchen table
and Carla notices her eyes are closing.
Would you like to take a nap?
Carla asks. *You can lie down on this bed*

(23)

Cloaked. Shielded
from whatever
is oncoming

(24)

It's still light out
It's a June afternoon
Come, Carla says to her son,
let's go into the other room.
Let's let Isha sleep.
We'll just be in the living room, Carla
says to Isha, gently closing the swinging door
to the kitchen. She
has given Isha a quilt
she's just folded from the laundry basket

(25)

I will not call the police.
If someone comes to my door asking for shelter
will I offer it, though it endanger me?
There are precedents for this:
When I was at Simona's in Vicopisano
she showed me the false ceiling
over the second floor of her house
where her grandparents hid Jews
and *partigiani*
during the war.
A space so narrow they had to lie on their stomachs

(26)

I am sheltering this woman, Carla
says to herself (Isha is sleeping
a long time. Quietly, as she did
when her children were small,
Carla walks back into the kitchen,
looks in the fridge
for something to make for dinner),
*though I know people will tell me
I shouldn't.* And even myself—
will I ask myself *Should I have done this?
Have I endangered myself, my children?*
The woman a stranger, possibly psychotic,
possibly being followed because
she has done something
I should be afraid of.
I am a single mother with two children
whose father will not approve.
My friends, or most of them,
will not approve. *How do you know
she hasn't exposed you all
to the virus?* Quietly, so as not
to wake Isha, Carla takes
some leftover tomato sauce
from the refrigerator. She looks
in the cupboard for pasta. Helicopters
circle overhead. *There are worse
things than viruses,* she says out loud.
But quietly enough so no one can hear her

(27)

Will, who is about to graduate from fifth grade,
lies on his stomach on the living room floor
folding a piece of green construction paper.
You've got enough, Carla says.
You've made one for everyone in your class.
They have counted carefully. The hats
all have names on them.
I know, Will tells her.
He has not seen even one of his classmates
in twelve weeks.
This one is for Isha when she wakes up

(28)

I am thinking of what it must have been like
to lie on your stomach
and wait out the Nazis
in an unlit space
beside others you couldn't see.
Whose breathing—
and the sounds of the family
living downstairs, going
about their days—
you listened to

(29)

Isha opens the kitchen door, walks into the living room

(30)

The teacher has come and picked up the hats
and there is one green hat on the coffee table
in front of the couch
with Isha's name on it

(31)

It has helped her to sleep.
Now Isha remembers her nephew's phone number.
Julie and Will are watching a movie.
Carla heats up pasta
from their dinner for Isha.
I think I feel better now, Isha tells her.
*If you'd call my nephew I think I could go
and stay with him*

(32)

What Elijah McClain was doing that night
on the streets of Auburn, Colorado,
was buying iced tea for his brother

(33)

Carla calls the number Isha has given her
and Isha's nephew answers.
I have no way to pick her up, he says, a helplessness
in his voice, and Carla says, *I will drive her.*
Isha puts on the green paper hat with her name

(34)

This is what happened. This is how it happened.
A woman knocked on a door and was afraid.
A fifteen year old girl saw no reason
not to let her come in. A ten year old boy
made her a hat like the ones she'd helped him make
for his classmates he couldn't be with.
This happened during a pandemic.
This happened after four hundred years
of violence and fear and being followed
happening and happening

(35)

Carla drives Isha to her nephew's and her children
stay at their house and wait. That's the way it ends.
That's almost the way it ends

(36)

Later the children will talk about Isha
and ask how she got to their house and why.
It's almost like she was a spirit, Will says. *Almost
like she didn't really exist and then she did
and then she didn't.* He thinks
for a minute. *A good spirit,* he adds

(37)

Carla and Julie and Will do not get the virus.
Elijah McClain is dead almost a year
before his whole story is told

(38)

Was Isha real? Was she
a ghost? Was she a fragment
of a truth
that waited and waited
before she found
the right door to knock on?

(39)

And this is not the whole story
It is never the whole story

(40)

Weeks later Carla will open the door and find a note.
Written in pencil, on notebook paper, with a drawing
of a folded hat and the names Will, Julie, Carla
on the front of the hat. *Thank you,*
the note says. No signature

Notes

Rabbi Hillel, born 110 BC, is known for the *Pirket Avod (Ethics of the Ancestors)* in the Talmud. This teaching in its entirety is as follows:

"If I am not for myself, who is for me? When I am for myself, what am I? If not now, when?"

Sandra Bland was a 28-year-old African American woman who was arrested for a supposed minor traffic violation and arrested. She was found hanged in her Texas jail cell three days later.

Elijah McClain was 23 when he was walking home on August 24, 2019, in Colorado. He was apprehended by police for being "suspicious," put in a carotid hold, and injected with ketamine. He had a heart attack and was declared brain dead. He was taken off life support and died on August 30.

Isaye Barnwell, of Sweet Honey in the Rock wrote the song that provides the title for the second poem in this book, "Would You Harbor Me."

About the Author

Anita Barrows was born in Brooklyn, New York, in 1947 and has lived in the San Francisco Bay Area since 1966. Among her awards in poetry have been grants from the National Endowment for the Arts, the Ragdale Foundation, the Centrum Foundation, and the Dorland Mountain Arts Colony, and publications by The Quarterly Review of Literature and the Riverstone Press. Her three poetry chapbooks from The Quelquefois Press in Berkeley are housed, among other places, in the University of California Library (Berkeley and Santa Cruz), the British Museum, and libraries in Baghdad and Kabul. She has had two previous books published by The Aldrich Press (Kelsay Books). Anita Barrows and Joanna Macy have collaborated on four translations of the work of Rainer Maria Rilke, including *Letters to a Young Poet,* and Barrows' novel *The Language of Birds* will be published by She Writes Press in 2022. She has also done translations since 1972 of novels, poetry, plays, and non-fiction from French and Italian. Barrows holds a PhD in psychology and is Institute Professor of Psychology at the Wright Institute, Berkeley. She maintains a private clinical practice in Berkeley and is a mother and grandmother and companion to a household of dogs, cats, and birds.

www.ingramcontent.com/pod-product-compliance
Lightning Source LLC
Chambersburg PA
CBHW071642090426
42738CB00013B/3188